First Light

For Emerging Poets

*

MINDSET

&

9 FAST-TRACK MODELS

Sally Naylor

Parson's Porch Books
www.parsonsporchbooks.com

First Light: For Emerging Poets

ISBN: Softcover 978-1-951472-07-8

Copyright © 2019 by Sally Naylor

All rights reserved. No part of this book may be reproduced or transmitted in any form or by any means, electronic or mechanical, including photocopying, recording, or by any information storage and retrieval system, without permission in writing from the publisher.

Cover Credit: Photo by Dr. Stan Johnson

Thanks

To all my Ransom Everglades and Baylor School students

To my buddies, my 3 grandsons: Max Monteith, Nathan & Jacob Naylor

To Blaise Allen and Meryl Stratwood for editorial input

To my teachers:

Jim Daniels, Campbell McGrath, Maxine Kumin & Tony Hoagland

For gifted colleagues at the Baylor School:

Jim Stover, Chris Watkins & Park Lockrow

who provide students with a safe space to learn and to thrive.

Dedicated to all those who avoid their own melodrama, "poor me," moral watchdog or sermonizing tendencies. Your writing supports compelling poetry. Thank you.

As Dickinson said, *Tell all the truth but tell it slant.*

TABLE OF CONTENTS

Overview and Mindset	11
The Naylor Method	33
Nine Models	35
Genesis	65
Open Letter to The Apprentice Poet	64
The Creative Process	71
"Drive-By Jesus:" Titles and Tips	73
A Sampler of Narrative Hooks	73
Ten Basics of Effective Writing	77
Rubrics, Checklists & Worksheets	83
Glossary of Literary Terms (Use it!)	90
Reading Lists	97
Author Profile	99

Doesn't everything die at last, and too soon? Tell me, what is it you plan to do with your one wild and precious life?

--Mary Oliver

OVERVIEW

Poetry arrived in search of me. I don't know, I don't know where it came from, from winter or river. I don't know how or when.
-- Pablo Neruda

This is a book about courage, the courage to make art, it's also about resilience, flexibility, risk-taking, creative writing and living, it's about clarity – how to inspire yourself and others, and how to follow your own muse as you learn to analyze, adapt and then reconfigure the strategies of master poets. It considers big picture concerns, yet it also works small. Giving and receiving candid and kind feedback in a workshop is also essential. It's a book about community and about showing up with the right tools.

Written by a poet-therapist, it's not for dummies or idiots, but for the clever, the adept, and for those ambitious enough to aspire to live in print. If you are frustrated or feel stuck because your growth is slow, opt for this method, these models. If you have a calling, as Donald Hall said, *to get the unsayable said*, the models will assist. A skill-building manual, *First Light* also has attitude; it is as feisty and ephemeral as poetry.

"*To say in words what can't be said in words,*" is my favorite definition of poetry. Acknowledge first that you have chosen to attempt the impossible. Realize that this challenge can overwhelm; the vulnerability and stamina required are exacting. And the wildly erratic nature of much of our early writing will sometimes appear to us to be mortifying. Yet, we write on. This workbook will assist you to do it more efficiently.

If you've ever wanted to be *delivered into the realm of pure song*, to step into the space of a master poet or to present a riveting reading and then head out to choose the cover for your next book, you have come home.

Master poets have created a series of odd legacies. Edgar Allan Poe wrote with "Catarina," his cat, on his shoulder, and Dame Edith Sitwell prepped by lying in an open coffin to get her creative juices flowing. Emily Dickinson never left home, while Whitman wandered the profligate public highways.

This workbook supports your own idiosyncrasies, but the Naylor Method is more mainstream or linear. It recommends a coherent process that draws on both the logical and creative realms as it inculcates the skill-building savvy required to avoid years of a grueling, non-productive apprenticeship without the risk of either coffin or cat allergies.

First Light offers a survey of the poetic landscape as well as the best compass: a faith in your own compass. While it won't create instant poetry or even coffee, it does provide a reliable fast track: an antidote for years of flailing. It also acts as a catapult or jumpstart. Your time and expertise will now be focused, as you part company with most rank beginners.

To achieve competency in any field an awareness of its intellectual and emotional landscape is required to insure success. If that awareness is combined with instruction in appropriate skills, and an easy-to-follow method and rubrics are also provided, *Voila!* Success. It sounds simple. And while it's easy to envision, it can be deceptively difficult to realize or to measure.

However, Lao Tzu warned, *if you do not change direction you may end up where you are going*. This text acts as blueprint for the necessary detours of your renewed energy. Emerging poets struggle with the frustrations of an admittingly daunting task. I often felt defeated as a young poet. I faced these difficulties again as a novice teacher of creative writing, and when I returned to writing, I wrestled with them a third time.

I realize now it's impossible to teach what you don't know; it also takes time to reverse engineer what you aren't quite sure you've mastered yourself. Persevere. This process grew primarily out of my frustrations with the vague and ineffectual "go home and write a poem" assignments that students receive from well-intentioned but clueless teachers. Even a good prompt does not provide any real structure or explicit directions.

Ignorance may be an acceptable excuse for those teachers, because, in their defense, crafting poetry is one of the most difficult language tasks available on the planet. Nonetheless, our teachers should be taught how, and not just what, to teach. And yes, I am available and eager to teach teachers. We can't all be poets. Writing competent poetry is challenging enough and it's especially difficult to identify, synthesize, replicate and then teach all the components of this expertise.

Here's a preview: The Naylor Method combines an initial reading of a well-crafted, published poem (See Chapter Three) which then provides the catalyst for a spontaneous free write. The emerging poet then considers the model provided, which lists step by step instructions: a sort of recipe. You are encouraged to incorporate at least 70% of the suggestions. Return then to your free write, highlight it, then weave any promising phrases or images that you culled from the free write into your rough draft. After the initial draft, evaluate it with a rubric, revise it again and then go on to employ the revision recipe. A final critique from a writing workshop is optional but tremendously useful. So to summarize: read, free write, follow the model, incorporate the free write into your draft, use the rubric, the revision recipe, and finally, get it workshopped. *Fini.*

Here are instructions for a free write. It's important to know that writing poetry is often more emotional than cognitive. Recognize also that the two are sometimes inextricable. This is where the value of a free write emerges. Just do it. Don't over think it. Fire your internal editor. Get out of your mind. Just dabble and play. Put your internal critic in time out. Surrender to your right brain. Flow. A free write is spontaneous, it isn't a logical or linear activity, it's a kind of taking dictation as your thoughts and feelings bubble up. Select a poem, topic or vivid memory as a catalyst. Be there. Step into it. Muse on its multiple aspects. Then

- Set a timer for seven minutes,
- Keep your hand moving, don't stop, don't edit, cross out or correct.
- If you can't think of anything to write, scribble, "I can't think of anything to write," until you do. Dive into your subconscious.
- Forget neat, forget grammar and spelling -- for now, scribble, lose control, take risks, write from the heart not the head, avoid logic – leap.
- If it helps, write with crayons or colored markers or with your left (non-dominant) hand. Order this disorder later.
- When the timer goes off, go back and highlight only the most vivid phrases or images, pull them out. Weave and incorporate the gems from your free write into your rough draft AFTER you follow the model.
- Get it out, spew forth, go out of your mind. Proofread and edit later.

It is essential that you consult the Glossary for terms with which you are unfamiliar. To learn any task, first master its vocabulary; this enables you to deconstruct, analyze and discuss it. And if you are currently feeling impatient, go ahead and skip to the first model, titled "Cicadas" in chapter three. Read it and then follow the instructions provided. If this assignment intrigues and/or produces some of the results you seek, then return to this introduction.

There is no inherent contradiction, between creativity and the use of pragmatic blueprints or recipes. But rather, merging the highest aspirations of the imaginative spirit with a practical methodology is mandatory, if you wish to save time and excel at any onerous task. My drive to unlock and demystify this process fueled *First Light*, the guide that my own younger self so much desired and needed.

The models in the body of this text provide recipes that improve your skills – they transform the inevitable difficulties encountered by any novice, who all experience what is known as "unconscious incompetence." Then move up to the next level: conscious incompetence. I expect that is where you are today. Your often clumsy, first experiments will, with the support of a model, and coupled with a practical right-brained process (like a free write) and an awareness of the advantages of an adaptive mindset, and a reliable rubric, will morph and finally evolve into the ease of a conscious and then finally an unconscious competency.

This metamorphosis can be experienced seamlessly, if you are willing to commit to a disciplined practice, but it is hardly inevitable. Unless you wish to wander aimlessly and endlessly in the woods as an apprentice poet, *live deliberately,* Thoreau advises. Your attitudes and mind-set are as important as your method or the habits that sustain them.

But first, recognize and celebrate that you are no longer out there, on your own. The models and method provided have been successfully employed by over eight hundred former students.

When we sallied forth they had never written a poem. Our work together usually spanned nine months and the students eventually netted an 85% publication rate. I've since worked with other students on a variety of levels and discovered that this process is suitable for any age and can be employed effectively by experienced wordsmiths.

Thank you for showing up for the nitty gritty! Yes, it can be fun, if you let it. When you finish *First Light*, please pass it on. You and your peers deserve many, many mentors and cheer leaders. Locate them. Ask questions. Then read.

I'd like to salute you for your bold, playful, indepenent, intrepid inclinations. They got you here. Now it is time to nurture yourself and benefit from and reinforce those strengths. And if the above traits don't describe you today, the mindset, models and method that follows will assist as you learn to live into and become better acquainted with each new version of your artistic self, as you try out and try on new expertise and personas.

Open the door a novice has arrived, is your welcome from the Persian poet, Rumi.

American poet Mary Oliver contributes her own lofty notion:

What I want in my life is to be willing to be dazzled – to cast aside the weight of facts and maybe even to float a little above this difficult world…. I want to believe that the imperfections are nothing – that the light is everything …. And I do.

Writing offers us the capacity to reinvent or transcend. The novelist Kurt Vonnegut provides input from a more pragmatic or prosaic realm -- that of the art of living well -- when he stated that being a writer allowed him to *edit himself into someone resembling an intelligent person.* That alone justifies your effort.

One of my own teachers, Jim Daniels, said the best advice he had for neophyte writers was to *have an interesting life*. Writing provides the space for firebrands who flame like Ginsberg, Sexton or Ferlinghetti, and also for the reticent, such as Dickinson.

Joy Harjo, native American poet, informs us: *as I write I create myself again and again.* Whether your tendencies lean towards the derelict, rogue or angst-ridden or you espouse a more introverted and intellectual approach or whether you fly as high as a jaunty, Whitmanesque bard -- whatever your mode or flavor, welcome!

This is a book of process not a compilation of narrow or one-dimensional writing prompts.

Models detailed in *First Light* provide opportunities to identify, clarify and morph personal stories, to lay claim to your own Phoenix narrative while employing the strategies of accomplished poets. In the exploration, you may change your story or locate another version or perspective as illustrated by the fine poem below.

NOT BAD DAD, NOT BAD

I think you are most yourself when you're swimming;
Slicing the water with each stroke,

The funny way you breathe, your mouth cocked

As though you're yawning.

You're neither fantastic or miserable

Getting from here to there.

You won't win any medals, Dad,

But you won't drown.

I think how different everything might have been

Had I judged your loving

Like I judged your sidestroke, your butterfly,

Your Australian crawl.

But I always thought I was drowning

In that icy ocean between us,

I always thought you were moving too slowly to save me,

When you were moving as fast as you can.

-- Jan Heller Levi

Time has provided this poet an opportunity to look through a different lens. So how to do you apply this insight to your own life? This poem is one of the models in chapter three: an epiphany poem.

We will start exploring models by reading and analyzing an example of fine poetry. Read the whole thing first, then digest it. Skip all prompts or exercises, initially, for they are too narrow. Model the whole. The poem is provided first. Then follow with a timed six-minute free write. Then incorporate the strategies suggested by the model, provided in an easy to follow list or recipe format.

Models provide short-term, informal apprenticeships, not to just one, but to a plethora of talented poets as you step out on your own, combining your own personal content with the techniques and strategies employed by master poets.

This is the first of several *First Light* volumes. Some day you will create your own models, at your own pace. And eventually, you will wean yourself. But this method coupled with a rubric and revision recipe will inevitably accelerate your progress. The final step is to join a workshop, then read and present your well-revised rough draft in order to benefit, finally, from the feedback of your peers.

An important early habit to cultivate is reading. My most enduring mentors were books. When I attended my first writing workshops, as I ventured out into the literary world, I was encouraged to read assiduously. Do not avoid it. Start now. Read contemporary American poetry -- not just the old guys. The suggested reading list at the back of this book provides a jump-start.

If you don't read contemporary poetry, you are literally ignorant of the environment in which you hope to thrive. Avoid time traveling. Get out of the 19th and 20th centuries. Stop parroting old poetess stereotypes or doing the old hip, rock star gig, replete with passe and predictable Dylan-esque, sing-along, sing-song Dr. Seuss-like lyrics. Rap too, or any other narrow path, type or poetic genre eventually restricts more than it frees. Don't skip the buffet and eat only burgers every day.

Go online and buy used books for mere pennies. Read, then read more. Continue to read, read, and then keep on reading. One of my mentors, advised me to avoid reading prose while I write poetry. This habit unconsciously educates your ear, then it easily and unconsciously, instills an appreciation for the virtues of concision and heralds your own ability to replicate it. When you are ready to write, rereading a handful of your most admired poets, also provides an inspirational catalyst. It may eventually feel like, on occasion, that you are only taking dictation, that the poem tends to write itself.

MINDSET: THE PSYCHIC LANDSCAPE

Let's now examine the poet's mental and emotional state. This landscape must be successfully negotiated and understood if we expect to hone techniques, develop skills, reproduce strategies, and then proceed to implement our own effective process. So let's explore the psychic territory of the poet and writer's landscape. Only then will the *atlas of this difficult world*, the one that I provided for former students, and which I now pass along to you, make any sort of sense.

This business of ... being a writer is ultimately about asking yourself, 'How alive am I willing to be?'

-- Anne Lamott

Writing is an apt metaphor for living. If you haven't paid your dues, haven't consciously lived or read, or lived merely in the shallows, it will be reflected in your work. Your audience will know, and you too, will know or at least, you may suspect, whether you are really in the game or just taking up space. Nourish yourself. Grow yourself, learn, then when you get yourself to the table, desk or a workshop, you will have something valuable to offer yourself and the world.

This is a book on craft, not bibliotherapy but the confessional impulse often acts as a trigger. I'm reminded of Picasso's quip, *Art is a lie that helps us understand truth*. Even though art means artifice, your truths will "out" as you write candidly. And while art has therapeutic aspects. Art is not therapy, and catharsis or lament is not necessarily healing or art.

The poem below suggests how to pursue your own truths. To decipher this poem, you should know that Sylvia Plath and Anne Sexton are the twin giants of confessional poetry and that catharsis means an extreme emotional purging. Again, consult the glossary if your knowledge of literary terms is sparse. It's all there.

TO PLATH OR TO SEXTON?

To bibliotherapy, that is the question.
To cathart or not to cathart? Dear writer,
your confessional may or may not be art,
but whatever else you do, ask, "Is it true?"
Try, then test its antithesis,
before you believe your own stories.
For words can shift your DNA, so savor,
& then live into a few other versions.

Suffering guarantees neither punch nor panache.
So let it all be metaphor, for Hamlet today, may
be Gertrude tomorrow, a cage is a cage
no matter how sweet, even those of your own construction.

Eckhart Tolle reminds us that *life is an adventure not a package tour* and that *For a problem to exist you need time and repetitive mind activity.* You can also embrace and turn around most of your initial emotional reactions. Emotional issues can be denied, relived, reviewed, reintegrated, put to rest, defanged or accepted during the writing and revision process.

These "starter" attitudes about the writer's geography, in addition to the Naylor Method will shift you into a gratifying practice whatever your skill level or age -- whether you've accrued twelve or ninety candles on that next birthday cake.

Let's now consider the major stereotype emerging writers have contended with for decades. Ernest Hemingway maintained, *There is nothing to writing, all you do is sit down at a typewriter and bleed.* These are potent words, but they are a little too pat, a little too glib for my taste! For there are few insights and no art in the spewing of the dreck of your personal misery -- a simple bleeding out on paper. The "wound" is not inevitable! and even a bleed out can be a candidate for revision or the waste basket. Hemingway was a literary giant not because he was wounded, but in spite of it. You do not have to commit suicide to pay your dues.

One of my students once expressed shame, as she showed me one of her journal entries. I encouraged her to value that sort of cathartic writing, for it does have a limited, initial emotional benefit; however, I agreed that the entry wasn't yet art, but that it is simply a matter of how much time she wished to devote to revision. It's possible to turn therapeutic writing into effective poetry or prose. It's important to know the value of each and be able to tell the difference.

How do you know the difference? Ask yourself if your writing is hyperbolic. Is it art or therapy? Does it whine or blame? Is it angst-ridden? Do you cast yourself as a victim? If so, trash it.

Hemingway revised the last page of *A Farewell to Arms* twenty-seven times. That fact may account for much of his literary dexterity, but his alcohol use, supported by the tendency of his peers in the "Lost Generation" to hang out in bars, predisposed him (and them) to alcoholism, depression and suicide.

His repellant (to me) bleed-out metaphor for writing, does not support good mental health or effective writing. That is the take-away of the Hemingway story. Writers are not required to fall into inextricable vats of agony. They can be honest, and yes, even happy, while exploring any sort of material. So choose your metaphors with care. Neuroscience informs us that thoughts create our realities. You might also wish to ask what sort of reality you wish to construct for yourself and your readers.

Many fine poets can spell the word fun and many even use their inevitable hurdles as an impetus to explore, clarify and celebrate the human spirit. Suffering alone is neither glamorous, sophisticated nor especially aesthetic or artistic and it's vastly overrated; it's a pose, too often adopted by the limited or merely ignorant – by those unaware of their options or those unable to change their metaphors – writing might just be a playground and not a bleed out. You decide. What feels lighter? Where do you want to live?

Instead of Hemingway's hyperbolic, melodramatic bleed out, I prefer Frost's analogies: *A poem begins as a lump in the throat, a sense of wrong, a home sickness, a love sickness.*

And I would also couple that insight with this thought by Rumi. *There are a hundred ways to kneel and kiss the ground. There are a hundred ways to go home again.* Poetry is one of those ways. And you can create your own compass, eventually.

Acknowledge that it's your reptilian brain's job to keep you safe and scan for danger -- sometimes with a fierce vigilance. Thank it! The brain reminds you to look both ways when you cross the street. Then realize that while its intentions may be good (to save your life) a constant stream of negativity does not often help. For (whatever it is) is usually not a life or death or a flight or fight situation, unless you choose to believe the fears, which may then proceed to make you sick or will almost certainly, demoralize you, if you let them.

What to do? Embrace the message. Then remember that the best way to discourage yourself is to naively believe all your mind's fear-based input and hysteria. Beliefs are often rooted in ancient cultural or family norms. They may have little or nothing to do with you. Be amused by the mind's latest negative stories and propaganda.

Then recognize that it may be the voice of your third grade teacher or your high-strung, Great Aunt Lucy talking in your head; it may be your Dad or brother, but it's not the voice of who you really are. Be aware. Question. Ignore it. Forgive it. Then forget it.

Or learn to enjoy being harassed as you become your Aunt Lucy's, Dad's or big brother's favorite puppet.

Ironically, for those who can weather the initial shocks, just the act of scribbling, of facing your demons, and transforming them into an artistic expression, often exorcises them. But it also sometimes anchors in a fear-based reality that isn't realistic or warranted. It is often appropriate to step back and simply disbelieve the mind IF it sends you *only* a steady stream of primarily dreary, low-down, soap-opera signals.

There is also a wisdom in being able to *find the ache and make it sing* as Tyler Knott Gregson advises. Better yet, write that ache and then take a walk. Today's world would benefit from scores of contemporary poets, with their own feisty voices, sharing their own versions of Whitman's *Song of Myself.*

Do your art and then forget labels or judgements; embrace your shadow self and your light, for they often intersect. They share the same body, mind, and spirit. And if you desire real clarity, seriously, don't take yourself (your mind or emotions) too seriously.

That is our paradox, for as Vonnegut said, *When I write I feel like an armless legless man with a crayon in his mouth.* Have some fun with that crayon.

Then crank it out, revise, get it to a good workshop where you will get feedback from kind and candid peers whose minds are also engaged in taking names and kicking butt. Support yourself. Support them too. Know that we all write a lot of junk. Be at peace with that. And when you do judge yourself, negatively, forgive yourself for judging.

Implementing the input of your peers in a workshop is vital, but change only what feels right to you. Consider this comment by yogi Aurodindo, *you carry within yourself all the obstacles necessary to make your realizations perfect.* Use those obstacles to realize your truth or light and your art and cultivate your own sense of humor. Life is hilarious.

Consider joining me for an interactive workshop adventure. Combine this guide with an online workshop. In this environment, you will learn to master the practice and protocols necessary to sustain a community. Many novices, like you, also wish to give back, as they learn.

Writing provides opportunities to recognize and then to exorcise nearly any psychic maladies. It's cheaper than therapy and won't provide you with someone else's (the therapist's) version of your story – along with their vague, dubious, one-dimensional or negative labels. Letting go of your old stories after writing them can be a soothing process, for as McCluggage asserts, *hanging on is the only sin.*

Poetry in Greek means to make. So why not play as you construct your lyrical Lego or twirl your verbal hula hoops, developing an attitude of *leap and the net will appear?* And when the net doesn't appear, for sometimes, it doesn't, embrace failure and fear and learn that they too, have benefits.

One of the more ironic blessings of my own life was what I learned during months of cancer treatment eight years ago – that facing challenge or death can wake us up and help us see with new eyes. Crisis is a great clarifier. It provided the catalyst for my first book. As Thich Nhat Hanh reminds us, *No mud. No Lotus.*

I would also argue that *"How Alive am I willing to be?"* is a useful question for truck drivers and florists as well as poets. For life is too precious to simply idle along.

One of my colleagues related once that he was worried that my students might be writing "too much poetry." He was concerned that their expository writing skills might suffer. He later reported that their poetic practice had in fact, improved their verbal competency.

For good writing is good writing whether it's labeled a college essay, an ode, flash fiction, blog post, elegy or satire. Genre satisfies the mind's need to categorize and put complicated ideas into a "proper" box. But is anything really that easy or simple?

Writing demands we confront uncertainty each time we stare at a blank page; this holds true for the Nobel Prize winner and the rookie alike. That is the joy and dread of it. No guarantees. You don't have to be a sky diver to experience fears and highs.

However, there are also centuries of legacy, many reliable mentors, and scores of common sense guidelines, both formal and informal. This workbook provides an overview or atlas with plenty of bread crumbs scattered along the way, including a set of operating instructions. And you will provide the compass.

Enjoy this jumpstart for your practice whether you are a novice or have merely stalled or are simply ambitious for more challenge. It is your job to grapple. Get used to it!

Locate your own epiphanies and share them. For writing offers more than the gratification of creating and recreating ourselves in isolation. It is also community. A community that often appreciates three great action verbs. Create. Love. Play.

THE NAYLOR METHOD

It's not the strongest of the species that survives. Not the most intelligent that survives. It's the one that is most adaptable to change.
 -- Charles Darwin

- Select a model. Read it. Do a six minute free write, then a cluster brainstorm.
- Write a rough draft. Utilize over 70% of your model's tips & instructions.
- Proofread for plagiarism! Use *only* strategies & techniques, not the exact words.
- Incorporate best phrases from free write & your cluster brainstorm into the draft.
- Then evaluate with the Rough Draft Rubric. Revise again.
- Read aloud.
- Fill out the Revision Worksheet and Revision Recipe.
- Revise again. Incorporate only the feedback that feels right.
- Read aloud, again. Tweak it. Share your piece. Take it to a workshop.
- Revise again & submit for publication.

Darwin's thoughts about flexibility inscribed above, also extend to the act of writing. This method works due to its opportunity for endless interplay – for feedback, flexibility and adaptability; it enables you to tinker and compose until your words morph easily into the poem they were meant to be. Enjoy the odyssey.

NINE

MODELS

TYPES OF MODELS

We'll explore several types of models or stereotypical compositions. Do not follow any one recipe exactly, this exploration is intended to stimulate your own thinking and to provide some direction and a few examples. Poetry is replete with literary strategies you can mimic. I'm not interested in making this a long and onerous read, so I'll skip *The Odyssey* and other book length poems and will provide, instead, concise poetry. We will work small and hone our skills. Many of these strategies also work well in prose.

One concern some have shared with me is the point of view that using a model is equivalent to plagiarism. This approach does **not** invite plagiarism; it merely provides a list of successful devices and strategies, because whether consciously or unconsciously, we inherently parrot much of what we have already heard or read. Modeling tactics is much more straightforward and suitable as well as more fun than old pedestrian attempts to steal as we paraphrase and then duplicate ideas, ripping off someone's exact words. We will employ only strategies or tactics incorporated by accomplished poets, **not** their exact words. We simply utilize their techniques and shape them to our own content.

Last week I fashioned a fine poem by using two words that intrigued me after having read a poem by a friend of mine; our themes, tones and ambitions were different, all the language was different -- except for the two shared words; we both mentioned the words Eden and longitude. That is not plagiarism! That is one of the benefits of being inspired by another and admiring another's result enough to employ his/her strategies. This process acts as a catalyst for creativity when properly applied; however, it is also important to acknowledge that any process or method can be abused or corrupted.

MODEL #1: BUGGED? NATURE AS EXTENDED METAPHOR

Enjoy this charming piece by Jeffrey Delotto and the accompanying model, then create your own lively insect poem or try a prose sketch.

CICADAS

There's something so George C Scott
about a cicada, looking like a helmeted
tank commander rolling inexorably forward,
up and out at seventeen years underground,
years of barreling in darkness, of nursing
sweet sap from swollen-breasted roots, of
isometric flexing and pumping hydraulic
fluids beneath a brown-husked placenta
carapace....

A diesel among insects, he buzz-rumbles
up into my hard-shell pecan, singing the
dry hundred-degree evening for a moment's
bliss, a moments kiss of death, before tumbling
to the concrete, a file of ants marking the spot
next morning as his lover prepares her eggs
for the allure of the cooling darkness.

Oh, armored harbinger, what new world
will your children know, what new sun rise in that time?

THE INSECT (OR SCIENTIFIC RESEARCH) MODEL

- Title the piece with the specific name (scientific or Latin) of an insect.

- Do some research. Know your bug. Include at least seven to ten facts.

- Use an historical or literary allusion to describe the insect. In this case it is the actor who played the movie role of General Patton: "*George C. Scott.*"

- Use ordinary language but upgrade your diction: as in *"inexorable"* or "*harbinger*"

- Use parallel structure. Repeat the same grammatical constructions: ie repetition of ING words: *borrowing, nursing, flexing, pumping*. Note that a list of verbals, ie. *flexing*, is grammatically apt for a long, passive, seventeen-year hibernation.

- Use a simile "*looking like a helmeted tank commander.*"

- Employ alliteration*: "sweet sap*" & "*swollen*"

- Use vivid visual imagery: "*a file of ants"* include color (brown) & action (flexing)

- Employ metaphor: "*a diesel among insects*"

- Describe the environment: "*pecan tree, the hundred degree heat*"

- Create hyphenated words like *buzz–rumbles, brown-husked,* & *swollen-breasted*

- Add synesthesia, mix the senses as in "*singing the hundred-degree evening*" A/K

- Try personification as in *"kiss of death."*

- Use anaphora as in "*What new world, ... & what new sun*"

- Conclude with two questions & suggest an image of future: "*What new sunrise?*"

MODEL #2: INITIATION

Initiation always involves a coming of age story. Here Yusef Komunyakka explores the psyche of a child disturbed by learning more than he needs to know at an early age.

VENUS'S FLY-TRAP

I am five, wading out into the sunny grass,

unmindful of snakes & yellow jackets,

out to the yellow flowers quivering in a sluggish heat.

Don't mess with me because I have my Lone Ranger six-shooter.

I can hurt you with questions like silver bullets.

The tall flowers in my dreams are big

as the first State Bank and they eat all the people

except the ones I love. They have women's names

with mouths like where babies come from.

I am five. I'll dance for you if you close your eyes.

No peeping through your fingers.

I don't suppose to be this close to the tracks.

One afternoon I saw what a train did to a cow.

Sometimes I stand so close I can see the eyes of men

hiding in boxcars. Sometimes they wave and holler for me to get back.

I laugh when trains make the dogs howl. Their ears hurt.

I also know bees can't live without flowers.

I wonder why daddy calls Mama honey? All the bees in the world live

in little white houses except the ones in these flowers.

All sticky and sweet inside. I wonder what death tastes like?

Sometimes I toss the butterflies back into the air.

I wish I knew why the music in my head makes me scared.

But I know things I don't supposed to know.

I could start walking and never stop.

These yellow flowers go on forever.

Almost to Detroit. Almost to the sea.

My mama says I'm a mistake. That I made her a bad girl.

My playhouse is underneath our house,

and I hear people telling each other secrets.

-- Yusef Komunyakaa reprinted from *Magic City*

COMING OF AGE MODEL FOR VENUS'S FLYTRAP

Drawing on your own content and tone, select ten of the fifteen strategies below. Compose your own original poem as you incorporate Komunyakaa's techniques.

- Select botanical term as a title that reflects or sets tone or acts as a symbol.
- Adopt the persona of a young child. State, *"I am ____."* Fill in the age.
- Create a dialogue with an imaginary other.
- Describe the natural details of the environment.
- Use an allusion to a historical figure like the *Lone Ranger.*
- Mention the name of a specific toy.
- Refer to several characteristics of the title plant or flower.
- Use a simile: *"language like bullets."*
- *No _____.* (Mention a rule)
- Use age appropriate grammatical mistake: *"I don't supposed to know."*
- *I wonder_____?* Ask a series of questions? *"What does death taste like?"*
- Include more natural description or geography.
- Repeat the question with *I wonder what* an abstract noun: death, love, shame, Or honor, looks, tastes, feels, or sounds like?
- Reveal a secret. (*"I made Mama a bad girl"*)
- Use dialogue: Mama says_____. *"I made her a bad girl."*

Here is a list of plants.

Sweet William, Love-Lies-Bleeding, Viper's Grass, Bitterroot, Queen Anne's Lace, Baby Blue Eyes, Slime Mold, Toadstool, Wallflower, Mint, Vetch, Adder's Fern, Forget-Me-Not, Dahlia, Dogwood, Narcissus, Cockscomb, Candytuft, Foxglove, Fleur-de-lis, Hart's Tongue, Oleander, Morning Glory, Moccasin Flower, Mimosa, Violet, Bluebell, Black-Eyed

Susan, Bachelor's Button, Snowdrop, Sunflower, Sweet Pea, Indian Corn, Sugar Cane, Timothy, Wild Oats, Liverwort, Mustard, Parsley, Sage, Wisteria, Zinnia, Snowdrop, Bracken Amaryllis, Anemone, Cows Slip, Monkshood, Crocus, Daffodil, Lupine, Lady's Slipper, Jonquil, Hollyhock, Rock Weed, Hibiscus, Azalea, Poinsettia, Buttercup, Cactus, Fireweed, Indian paintbrush, Carnation, Columbine, Edelweiss, Gardenia.

MODEL #3: EPIPHANY

This model consists of relating an experience or situation from which you gain insight or learn something of value. But first some advice for beginners:

NOT TRENDING: THE BIBLIOTHERAPY GAME

When young, I wrote about my red neuroses,
bled out in scribbled journals:
so bloody wounded, so confessional and artistic.

Today I find the stories: making of meanings,
the striving for significance, my trying on
Plath and Sexton's black suicide boots,
a dreadful model – and that old need
for pathos and adoration: boring.

So poets, remove your heads from that oven.
It's not even good therapy, this rewinding
of dreck to perpetuate purportedly cathartic wallows.

For the "get it all out" school, feels much like
stoking a fire or some neophyte engineer's
phase-locked oscillator, stuck in recycle, recycle. Recycle.
Suffering on paper does not necessarily constitute art.

"NOT TRENDING" MODEL

- Write a hyperbolic soapbox or op-ed poem. Sell your point of view.

- Use contemporary diction like trending & contrast it with an older practice.

- Employ a color word to describe an abstraction *(red neurosis)*

- Use metaphor. *(bled out)*

- Employ anaphora. *(so bloody wounded, so confessional...)*

- Metaphor & symbolism. *(black suicide boots)*

- Refer to literary/historical allusions (*Plath & Sexton*)

- Use rhyme. *(adoring, boring)*

- Contrast dark theme with upbeat light-hearted ironies and tone.

- Apostrophe (use a direct address or command as in *"So poets, ..."* or as e e cummings says, *"Humanity, I hate you...."*

- Then use another allusion, *remove your heads from that oven.* This is a reference to how Plath killed herself.

- Like an investigative journalist, don't be afraid to criticize or use satire.

NOT BAD DAD, NOT BAD

I think you are most yourself when you're swimming;
Slicing the water with each stroke,
The funny way you breathe, your mouth cocked
As though you're yawning.

You're neither fantastic or miserable
Getting from here to there.
You won't win any medals, Dad,
But you won't drown.
I think how different everything might have been
Had I judged your loving
Like I judged your sidestroke, you butterfly,
Your Australian crawl.
But I always thought I was drowning
In that icy ocean between us,
I always thought you were moving too slowly to save me,
When you were moving as fast as you can.

                         -- Jan Heller Levi

MODEL FOR NOT BAD DAD, NOT BAD

- Use several types of visual imagery, limit the activity or perspective. (swimming)

- Be specific. *(mouth cocked)*

- Use simile. *(like yawning)*

- Define a person through an activity.

- Make a neither/nor statement about activity/person. (*fantastic or miserable*)

- Clarify statement with specifics, in this case *win medals or drown.*

- Ask how could your insight, attitude or conclusions have made things different?

- Use the technical diction of your chosen activity (swimming) with specifics like *Australian crawl, butterfly, side stroke*

- Employ antithesis like *fast/slow.*

- Use repetition and rhyme in title.

- Create an insight that changes the fundamental nature of the relationship: i.e. the father was doing the best he could, due to his own handicaps.

MODEL #4: THE CHARACTER SKETCH

Introduce an influential and/or colorful character. Try describing a family member. Avoid heavy-handed moralizing or preaching. Well-chosen details make your points for you. Select your anecdotes well and you can show and then you won't tell, or bore your readers. I include a character sketch of Alfredo, a stranger who shared his story with me; the model or recipe follows.

THE ALWAYS I LOVE YOU ALFREDO SONG

Fourteen years now -- gone from Miami; it's a kind of homecoming,
after an exile sequestered on mountains,
this serving up of black beans & pork, plantains fried big as pancakes,
I eat on the patio & scan the mural of an old *Havana* fort,
maybe *San Carlos de la Cabana*.

No music tonight, til after hours, when Alfredo picks up his guitar,
seats himself two feet away & serenades:
the melody, the Spanish timbre, the all you need to know
of the full-throated warble of melancholy:
nostalgia as only a Cuban can voice it.
& then the stories: how he slept in a car while working three jobs
how his Russian came in handy while settling refugees in Seattle
& the "rude" American social worker he married,
the photos of his children: two boys, all after he left Havana,

after the execution of his father, the doctor,

after he left med school, became a pilot, after he flew out

twenty-two relatives and forty-four others (how there are no secrets in Havana, the relatives told friends, who then showed up at the airport) and landing in *Mayami,* making his way to Melbourne, Florida, eventually, where his framed pilot's uniform hangs in the foyer of *El Ambia Cubano* which is how he came to be serenading us at eleven pm on the patio and yes, he painted the mural. I have never known your language, Alfredo, yet I can receive its possibilities. But I have known you before, somewhere, somehow -- shining through myself & others – a stranger, giddy & in communion – as that truth rings its final bell: *siempre, t'amo, Alfredo.*

--Sally Naylor Reprinted from *Riffs*

THE CHARACTER SKETCH MODEL

- Describe an interaction with a fascinating individual.

- Compose a long title.

- Frame the piece with two refrains, one in the title and one at the end. Use two languages. In this instance one is in English the other Spanish.

- Include four or five plot incidents. Use lists. Retrace a journey.

- Use snippets of another language or substitute the specialized diction or jargon of the topic you explore, i.e., "phase locked oscillators," if exploring engineering. Try a mechanic's lingo, the dog trainer's "heel, sit or stay" or explore the ballerina's tutu, plie or pirouette.

- Explain the fascination. Do not attempt to be entirely coherent. Try to say in words what can't be said in words. Try magic. (If it doesn't work, delete it. Nothing lost.)

- Use a visual image as a symbol or metaphor. (the uniform in the restaurant foyer)

- Pepper the piece with details of location: geography, food, patio, flatland, mural, music. Include visual, auditory and kinesthetic imagery. Research: Cuban fort.

- Include oddities, foibles *"rude" American social worker*, pet peeves. Quote them.

- Combine poetic lines in regular stanzas with a prose poem stanza.

- Have fun. Fall in love. Play. Make yourself and the world cry. Simmer overnight, then bake at 250 degrees revise for two hours. Done.

Another variation on the character sketch is the elegy.

ELEGY FOR JIM HATCH

I was taxed by your ill-timed, bawdy innuendoes
in mock-falsetto whispers, by your obesity and bad teeth.
I leaf through your copy of *The Art of Eating,*
a dog-eared volume offered as compensation
for your vaunted caviar pie, the one you never
got around to making. I loved you anyway. This bookmark
half hides the chapter on "How to be Cheerful Though Starving."

It's the handmade label from a jar of sweet & sour tarragon mustard,
contents: eggs, sugar, mustard, vinegar,
dated 6/5/89, signed Jim. Red-headed, piquant
like your cooking, you were an anarchy that believed
in institution: this book, that label and a note
in your hand is all I have left. You wasted away
so quickly: died dirty and alone in Italy.
Not even Byron would have thought it romantic.

Yet I hear you wrangle still with your correct
Princetonian, Episcopal God, having cooked and kept your wolf
at bay for fifty years. Sleep well, old sweet and sour.

-Sally Naylor Reprinted from *Dry Creek Review* & *Heresies and Sweet Basil*

ELEGY (OR EULOGY) MODEL

- Write a wry, honest modern elegy or eulogy. Capture the whole human being.
- Incorporate specificity:
  Include dates, education, religious affiliation, book titles, chapters, quotations.
- Select an object that can be used as an extended metaphor for the person
  As in Chapter on *"How to be Cheerful though Starving"*
- Employ images: sound, *falsetto whispers* & visual. *Red-headed, obese.*
- List both foibles as well as virtues. List many specifics. You can always delete.
- Rewrite a cliché: *cooked and kept your wolf at bay*
- Use antithesis=*sweet & sour.*
- Allusion= *Lord Byron*
- Define the subject with an abstraction, use antithesis or paradox, then personify it as in *"an anarchy that believed in institution"*
- Describe details of the physical decline
- Say farewell in a conversational tone. *"Sleep well."*
- Avoid excessive sentimentality, while embracing clear-eyed affection.

MODEL #5: THE "HOW TO"

Teaching can be a lively way to get educated and to entertain. I've include here one of my eighth-grade student's poems from The Baylor school, Logan Funderburk, and what I consider to be a rather clear, clean, concise, nifty and bold piece of work. Below is his "How To."

HOW TO LAUGH LIKE A MAD SCIENTIST

The key to laughing like a mad scientist is in the diaphragm. This is where the sound starts. The first step: inhale deeply, like Doctor Frankenstein, until you could be popped like a balloon. Then release the air to form a MWA sound. After the first MWA, you expel five steady HA's and then repeat from MWA, only louder. MWA, HA, HA, HA, HA, HA. Then repeat this series and on the last HA, hold the sound, letting it resonate. While doing this, rub your hands together and then raise your hands in the air and tilt your head back. MWA, HA, HA, HA, HA! Stop and try this for a while. If there are people you don't like around, it might scare them away. Now you are certified to laugh like a mad scientist. The next chapter details how to become a mad scientist.

--Logan Funderburk

INSTRUCTIONS FOR WRITING A "HOW TO"

- Select a ludicrous situation: mad scientist. Avoid boring topics. Have fun.
- Supply the key or answer the big question. In this prosaic poem the key equals the use of your diaphragm.
- Use a simile and at least one allusion, *"Doctor Frankenstein."*
- Incorporate sounds: like "*MWA, HA HA HA*"
- Name steps – at least three.
- Use commands. Instruct the reader with authority.
- Adopt an informal tone by using you -- second person.
- Combine visual & auditory imagery. Rub hands and tilt head back.
- Create and include a certification.
- Specify the next step(s).

Many students revel in this prompt. I have essays on how to steal from your neighbor's wine cellar and how to survive cellblock nine. It might even be fun to instruct your reader about how **not** to write a college essay or get a prom date.

Another variation of the "how to" assignment could be a recipe or food poem:

CALIENTE

Nostrils flare and eyes tear
as air testifies to the pungency of peppers,
secure in sounds of smooth steel on wood,
in the inexorable chopping of spheres.

Sliced green chilies and tomatoes chopped thin,
then add scallions, a dozen black olives--large,
jalapenos--slice; one soft avocado--dice;
scissor fresh cilantro and sprinkle in.

Finish off this evolving salsa,
this potion of mine, with a bite
of fresh garlic and one dwarf lime.

Accept this offering from my odd kitchen.
An import from alien territories,
a mixture, concocted for its hot delight,
all stimulant and healing,
taken for the burning away of demons.

--Sally Naylor, Reprinted from *Texas Poetry Calendar* and *Firebird*

MODEL (RECIPE) FOR A FOOD POEM

- Employ cookbook diction: use words like sauté, simmer, marinate, boil, whisk, sizzle, spice, dice, mince, smother, scramble, chop or top.

- Use a recipe format.

- Try personification, as in *"the air testifies"* or a metaphor like *"an alien import."*

- Experiment with point of view.

- Make the piece a gift or a letter or tell it from the point of view of the food. Personify food. Make it shy or hot, give it hands or eyes.

- Do not neglect the auditory: play with rhyme as in *dice, slice and bite*.

- Employ alliteration such as *"secure in sounds of smooth steel."*

- Incorporate paradox such as *"all stimulant and healing."*

- Employ the senses of smell and taste.

- Leap from the concrete to the abstract: *"our dreams may drink coffee with us."*

- Employ linked metaphors: *"this table has been a house in the rain and an umbrella in the sun."* This example comes from another food poem.

- Speak with authority. Use commands. Use action verbs like *"scissor."*

Below is another food poem, a prose poem with an entirely different tone and intention. Try analyzing and constructing you own model from this poem. Then follow it.

PERISHABLES

In the final days of the war, a boy eats cake, a cake from the saddest mother, a woman unaware that her own son has bled into history, a history with jaws that are soft and tropical, the greenest green, not gray like Lake Erie in winter.

The cake sealed first in waxed paper, then gift wrap, then a grocery bag dismantled with pinking shears, the bundle tied with cotton string, her fingers recalling the tiny buttons of his school shirts, the comb dipped in water before parting his hair.

Mercy rains at every latitude, at each contested parallel, rains anywhere that grunts line up for salt pills, clean socks, for unclaimed parcels that go to those who never get mail.

Cake sweetens the mouth of a boy the woman will never meet, a boy who tastes in the kindness of strangers the complications of survival, a boy who in manhood will crumble each time he tells the tale.

-- Holly Iglesias, reprinted from *Angles of Approach*

MODEL #6: THE PROSE POEM

First developed in the 1890's by Jean Valery, the prose poem did not become popular in this country until the 1960s and 70s. There is no listing for the prose poem in a handbook of literary terms published in 1936, but it is listed in the 1981 addition of that same book. Because it lies in that gray area between genres, it suited the mood of the outsider or disenfranchised. Immigrant workers, those protesting Vietnam, feminists and those concerned about civil rights, experimented with the prose poem. Latin American elements of magical realism are frequently but not always employed.

Other characteristics:

- It incorporates colloquial language, occasional use of second person,
- The right-hand margin is justified;
- It creates a continuous flow of detail, is very dense, but it moves quickly, with considerable momentum, which results in a breathless, run-on sentence quality;
- It employs frequent use of satire or social commentary,
- And is characterized by hypnotic sounds, incantations, repetitions or anaphora.
- Narrative elements are fragmentary and nonlinear or collage-like.

In the following piece, I write about place and to do it well, I break my own rule. I don't avoid hyperbole, but employ it, since it seems essential to convey the over-the-top energy of New York City.

SUGAR, SALT, LIFE

I'm at Don Giovanni's waiting for my *insallata frutta del mare dulce*, sitting in full sun, and it's joyful to say it with my college Italian intact, so much more vibrant, less effete than the French, while preposterous dog twins –- two sets -- trot by, walking their owners. I've come from my Guardian Angel. Captured her image on my iPhone, the real deal hangs regally in *bas relief* from the façade of the Guardian Angel Church in Chelsea, I flew up to her, slipped into her skin, and continued my trek, within half a block I spy the art guy with a truckload of large canvases and sense how easy it would be to live here, how this energy is me, the big me, the beyond the bright body of me or the temple of me, the possibility of me, the feist, vibration, contribution and vamp of me. And I say yes to New York without a plan. For I am grateful to your Sikh cab drivers in red turbans, to your Islamic women in their head gear wolfing down pastrami with their large bodies and families at Katz's. *NYC: tolerant of your beliefs & judgmental of your shoes*, declares a mini storage mural. I hear an Irish brogue and spot guys with dreads, a woman with nine-month baby belly sports Madonna heels. Oh Gotham, I am delirious -– you don't mess around. Neither do I. Time to exit stage left. Hear your chorus now: heal or die.

--Sally Naylor, Reprinted from *Rogue Nirvana*

Through my choice of details in this piece I reveal as much about myself as the city. I include next a rather unconventional prose poem, a kind of prayer as well as a road poem by one of my eighth-grade students, Catherine Scott. She, in turn, was modeling a prose poem by one of my teacher's, Campbell McGrath. I offer you a trilogy: my prose poem, "Sugar, Salt, Life" then my student's, "Road Music" and finally, my teacher's piece, "Sunset, Route 90."

ROAD MUSIC: 1-75, GETTING AWAY TO THE MIDDLE OF NOWHERE

We drove to be alone. To get away. To find ourselves. The music has harsh and heavy sounds, a rock steady beat, life pours out, filled with soul, filled with reflection, filled with knowledge, full of sound, the sound of drums and guitars, of chord after chord, the sound of that man singing his being out, sounds of clouds filling the fiery sky, sounds of the silence of Death Valley, sounds of understanding, sound that lets us know that others have come before, the sound of pain, of defeat, sounds of knowing that we can go back and get past it, sound of experience, sound of victory, of knowing we can come back in a few years and look back on this, sounds of hate, of love, of that hateful tough love that we receive too much of, sounds of solitude, of acceptance, the sound that shows us we must not accept life as it comes, sounds of fighting, of battle sounds of diving headfirst into the ocean from which we will surface, sounds like waves crashing on the walk. Sounds of wisdom, sounds of acquiring strength, the strength to forget, strength to move on, the strength to go back and pick up all the pieces. Sitting silently as we suddenly understand: sounds of hope, longing, love, life. Closure.

– Catherine Scott

And next, the model she used, written by my teacher, MacArthur "Genius" award winner, Campbell McGrath.

SUNSET, ROUTE 90, BREWSTER COUNTY, TEXAS

Now the light is brass and pewter, alloyed metals solid as Amber, allied with water, umber and charnel, lucent as mercury, fugitive silver, chalk rose and coal blue, true, full of the skulls and skeletons of moonlight, ash light and furnace light, West Texas whiskey light, bevel light, cusp light, light fall of arches and architectonics, earth light and anchor light, sermon light, gospel light, light that clasp hands with the few in the many, mesa light, saltbush and Longhorn light, barbed wire and freight train, light of the suffering, light of the desk fallen, weal light and solace light, graveyard at the crossroads light, floodlight, harbor light, light of the windmills and light of the hills, light that starts the dove from the thistle, light that leads the horses to water, light of the boon and bounty of the Pecos, light of the Christ of Alpine, light of the Savior of Marathon, Jesus of Cottonwoods, Jesus of Oil, Jesus of Jackrabbits, Jesus of Quail, Jesus of Creosote, Jesus of Slate, Jesus of Solitude, Jesus of Grace.

– Campbell McGrath reprinted from *American Noise*

Below is the model I created based on strategies employed by Campbell McGrath's "Sunset" poem. It was the model Catherine followed when she wrote "Road Music."

MODEL FOR A PROSE POEM: THE PRAYER, LIST AND/OR ROAD POEM

- In the title include time of day, highway, city, address, county or state.

- Use anaphora, refrain or repetition. Listen for a rhythm.

- Select a noun such as light and start a refrain with *"Now the light is ____ and ____, allied with _____, _____ and ____.*

- Play with syntax as in the phrase: *"blue, true"*

- Compare the light to a quotation such as, *"light that clasps hands with the few and the many."* Incorporate Shakespeare or the Bible or any source of elevated diction.

- Compare the light to a list of abstractions and then a list of specifics.

- Create hyphenated phrases like *"coal-blue or dusk-fallen"*

- Include real allusions or historical icons like *"boon and bounty of the Pecos,"* or *"Savior of Marathon"* or *"Christ of Alpine."*

- Then make up a few allusions of your own like *"Jesus of Cottonwood, Jesus of Jackrabbits and Jesus of Grace."*

- Use alliteration as in, *"the skulls and skeletons of moonlight."*

- As you conclude, substitute the keyword in your refrain or anaphora, such as light, to another word such as Jesus, or as Catherine does, leap from repeating the word *sound* to repeating *strength*.

WRAP-UP

The models will function as catalysts, your own versions, your own poetry, will echo or may, on occasion, resemble these models. That's ok, for this is your jumpstart, your debut. It is my conviction that if you employ these techniques and strategies and then work hard to make them your own, you will find success, as did my former students.

Models, the rough draft rubric and revision recipe will all expand your range, add energy and the "startle effect," if you are committed. It is my delight and compulsion to introduce you to good writing as a means of introducing you to your own inner muse. Write on. Then soar!

For those interested in publication, avoid vanity presses -- those who wish to charge you for publication. The quality is generally poor.

I suspect if you employ these models and work diligently, you too can enjoy publication, just one more way to build an impressive portfolio and demonstrate your panache, competence and drive. Consider it. Also make good use of the worksheets and checklists chapter. I'm delighted to hear from readers. Stay in touch. Let me know your victories, frustrations and publications.

If you are eager to experiment with more models look for my next workbook in this same format. Volume II will be published in 2020. Consulting for teachers or short trainings for creating and setting up your own workshops as well as individual instruction in writing your own models are also available. Work hard. And finally, if you aren't having fun, skip it.

GENESIS

Five years out of the classroom, after having spent time pursuing my own writing career, I returned briefly to teaching last March to assist a local private school who had lost a teacher mid-year. I taught three classes of English to high school juniors and seniors, who were designated as regular students, not honors or AP English students. This was the lowest level, and as I anticipated anemic or feeble motivation, I concluded that the successful creative writing curriculum I developed at the Baylor School in Chattanooga, Tennessee might help avoid lethargy: both theirs and mine.

Curious to determine if this same process would enable older students to either publish or write lively compositions, I was rewarded by their energy and meticulous work, and many did get published.

My approach was a dramatic departure from the rote, ho-hum, numbingly formulaic, expository writing that straight-jackets so many conventional high school students, a pedagogy which many teachers are currently required to parrot. I benefited from the freedoms extended by this school as well as those extended me by Baylor and Ransom Everglades Schools.

However, most traditional high school writing curricula is a left-brained sinkhole, fashioned from the stuff of boredom, made in a robotic wasteland destined to produce merely competent memo writers for some imaginary business or academic community.

And yes, the rest of the world thinks we're nuts. The "we" I refer to is the American language arts, mostly public school, educational system. The moronic "say what you are going to say, say it, and then say what you've said" mantra puts readers to sleep, as well as writers. Here is your wake-up call. If you want to jumpstart your writing, life or just dive into or deliver a compelling story or sketch in prose or poetry, modeling works.

Experiment with several of the models that first appeal to you, if you are keen for the practice that will enable you to become a more dynamic wordsmith. You will then go on to create long after this book has yellowed, been remaindered, deleted or shredded. Enjoy. Then fly!

OPEN LETTER TO THE APPRENTICE POET

The end. It worked well in grade four, but you'll need something a little more sophisticated to wrap up an effective personal essay or poem. Avoid the drab, the lazy or the conventional. As I mentioned earlier this is NOT a rehash of *the rote, ho-hum, formulaic, expository writing straight-jackets that many conventional high school students and teachers are required to parrot.* ...

You CAN have a beginning, middle and end without tedium. You can even parrot, but you do not need to do so monotonously, if you really wish to stay awake and entice your readers.

Make it clear. Make it bold. Make it brief. You can write and have fun. How? Use a model. Employ the strategies but not the content, tone, sound, format or diction of accomplished writers. Simply insert your own. As you use their techniques these tactics will slowly evolve into a tool kit that will constitute your own repertoire.

As a matter of fact, you already do this. Language acquisition involves listening and then reshaping the content of what you hear from family, friends and community and from what was read to you as a child.

For effective revision you need the skills of a practiced surgeon and the discrimination of a seasoned poet. William Faulkner's advice was *Slay your darlings!* Yes, it is daunting, but these are skills. They can be learned. And here are a few words on revision:

MUD PIES

I advise a novice to revise, to do it well,
first write on the head of an angel or pin.

Right it write or upside down. Invoke mud pie metaphor.
Locate some surreal playground. Dig deep.
Smooth your sticky patties, sculpt and pat as mud splatters.

Temper cravings for coronation in white space or by the academy,
divorce all errant longings for literary orgasm. Play.
Forget the Blake-Whitman transcendence tradition
or any hyper-scrupulous, gold-plated ostentation.

Slay your darlings, embrace, then discard the flawed.
Grab any passing, unmarried muse, Bunny Hop or Two-Step -- then Waltz,
Boogie-Woogie, Hockey-Pokey, Hully Gully, or Twist again, get down, get wonky

            then tango right off that set.

         --Sally Naylor reprinted from *Slay Your Darlings*

As you hone your work and evolve, go back periodically and review: The Naylor Method, The Creative Process, Ten Basics of Effective Writing and Worksheets & Checklists. Here are the fundamentals.

A mini-overview of basic writing principles and techniques represented in this guide include:

- ✓ Startle and intrigue in your introduction: use a hook!
- ✓ "Show don't tell."
- ✓ Be concise.
- ✓ Use parallel structure.
- ✓ Don't preach.
- ✓ Practice sentence variety;
- ✓ Vary the length, tone, structure, diction and complexity of sentences.

These tips keep you and your readers engaged. If this list confuses, don't worry. Read on. See the chapter on Ten Basics of Effective Writing for more detail. And finally know,

The Universe will not create for you what you are not willing to create for yourself.

-- Nikola Tesla

Up your game. Then raise your standards. I'm happy to help. Use the Rough Draft Rubric and get yourself a partner or ideally, locate a good workshop. Good writing delights as well as informs.

Ask yourself, am I having any fun, is my reader? Are you grappling with some universal human truth, do you offer an insight, a different slant or some closure? If not, trash, delete, recycle. Life is too short to be boring or settle for platitudes or the predictable. Mindset, models and process all matter, but don't kid yourself, so does work ethic.

And finally let me also echo and applaud David Ladinsky, author of *Darling I Love You,* who wrote:

The creation of art is a salvation in itself. When you make the pen dance, play an instrument with your soul, or excitedly talk about a project, the universe applauds. You bless the planet and all near when you are happy. Enthusiasm emits a fragrance we need. Adore what you can on this alter of miraculous existence, even during a dark night, everything is a magic lamp if you just know how to rub it.

THE CREATIVE PROCESS

The poem must resist the intelligence. /Almost successfully. -- Wallace Stevens

Part I. --The Creator

Take risks. Yes, I know risks are risky but without it writing is lackluster. After deciding on an appropriate topic, describe it. Seek specifics. List time, place, recall dialogue, other sounds, thoughts and details. Include the yellow railing with the peeling paint and the big Grundig radio on that porch. Try writing with your non-dominant hand. Draw the scene to stimulate memory. Write in present tense even if you describe the past, this makes the scene more immediate. Write it like a film. Use images. Employ a hook. Tell it quickly. Try a free write after drawing and then integrate. Get that first draft down, the raw emotion and detail. Ignore perfectionistic musings, spellcheck, revise *later*. Get out of your head; get into your heart. Pull out the best lines and images with a highlighter. And now, to change hats, we morph into our other friend,

Part II. -- The Critic

Type the poem. Put on your critic's hat. Print it. Get out your red pen. Look first for PVC: parallel structure, conciseness and sentence variety. Go over the Rough Draft Rubric and proofread for each item. Change verbs of being to action verbs. Avoid verbals and "ing" endings: both gerunds or participles. They are passive, not active, unless passive is part of your message. Count your images, then add a few more.

Incorporate more than just visual imagery. Add sounds, smells, feelings, tastes. Employ some figurative language and an allusion. Circle three drab or puny words and upgrade with a thesaurus. However, do not go thesaurus-mad. Speak in your own natural voice. Reread the conclusion. Does it provide a sense of closure? Do NOT merely repeat theme or thesis, extend your thinking.

Be fastidious about your conclusion. This is your last opportunity to affect your reader. Also search for appropriate epigraphs on sites like quotation.com. Read aloud. Listen for clunky sounds. Review the rough draft checklist and worksheet sections. Add. You can always delete. Better to have too much than too little in a rough draft. Next *Slay your darlings*. Delete the deadwood. Read for coherence and focus. Throw out any gems that are redundant or not relevant. Print. Read again. Recycle this process.

Part III. --The Performer

Let it simmer for at least a few hours, preferably days. Print and mark it up again. Read it aloud, again. Celebrate and locate a supportive listener or workshop. Listen to feedback but remember this poem belongs to you. Writing is not obedience training. Ignore input that doesn't work for you. Then revise again. You are almost home.

DRIVE-BY JESUS:

TITLES, OPENINGS, CLARITY, DICTION & MODELS

Always title your piece. Why? It's an opportunity. Why forfeit the opportunity to dazzle, add coherence or simply nail it with a pithy phrase? Just be sure it is pithy. To startle and to wake-up your reader are key functions of poetry, but so is clarity and appropriateness. Be clear and avoid alienating your audience.

I'd like to acknowledge a former student, Phil Zippes, who came up with the title, *Drive-By Jesus*; the poem he hoped to attach it to never did arrive, so thanks for the loan, Phil. I co-opted it, with his permission, for this mini-chapter on titles. I recommend that you too, also borrow and steal, and then acknowledge your sources.

While *Drive-By Jesus* does pass the startle test, it fails the alienation test, possibly offending devote Christians, which is why it wasn't the title of this book -- even though I was sorely tempted. Why? Confusion. This title has not yet been earned.

Challenge! If you can create something coherent and viable using this title, without alienating, please send me a copy, I'll include it in my blog. That would also please Phil. While his nimble diction combines worlds, mixing gansta jargon with conventional religion, what does it really mean? Where is he going? That's why Phil's poem never birthed itself. He just couldn't identify his focus, didn't know his own story. Who is driving this bus and why, are questions readers have the right and obligation to ask.

OPENINGS: A SAMPLER OF NARRATIVE HOOKS

Here are some examples of compelling hooks or opening sentences. They include examples of how to intrigue or tease your reader into your story. They stimulate your interest and capture your attention.

Like most boys in their teens, I wondered once in a while how I would take torture.

– Edward Hoagland

I particularly like New York on hot summer nights when all the…, superfluous people are off the streets.

– Gore Vidal

My father drank. He drank as a gut punched boxer gasps for breath, as a starving dog gobbles food – compulsively, secretly, in pain and trembling. I use the past tense not because he ever quit drinking but because he quit living.

– Scott Russell Sanders

One summer, along about 1904 my father rented the camp on a lake in Maine and took us all there for the month of August. We all got ringworm from some kittens and had to rub Ponds Extract over our arms and legs night and morning, and my father rolled over in a canoe with all his clothes on; but outside of that, the vacation was a success and from then on none of us ever thought there was any place in the world like that lake in Maine.

– E. B. White

For about fifteen minutes now I have been sitting chin in hand in front of the typewriter, staring out at the snow. Trying to be honest with myself, trying to figure out why writing this seems to me so dangerous an act, filled with fear and shame, and why it seems so necessary.

– Adrienne Rich

CLARITY

Read your piece as a skeptical observer. Pretend that you have not been part of this experience. As a stranger, would you have understood what was happening? Where are you in time and space? Who is the speaker? Does she/he have a discernible persona? Is the thesis/focus/theme clear? Do you support your message or ever re-examine it? Do the epigraph and title support your intentions? Can a bright eight-grader comprehend it? Is it too wordy? Consider the tone. Then evaluate with the Rough Draft Rubric.

DICTION

Its best to speak in your own voice and avoid pretentious or high-falutin' language. But I'd also circle three words that are dull and unimpressive and use a thesaurus to upgrade them. No need to sound like a PhD. dissertation. Ostentation alerts readers to suspect plagiarism when it isn't even warranted; most will not attribute it to simple pomposity. No one needs that kind of grief while working so hard just to sound pedantic or middle-aged – unless you are. Be yourself. Please. That is its own reward.

MODELS

Models are recipes, they provide structures or blueprints for composition. Anyone can learn to write models with a little practice. A gratifying way to start writing is to follow my models and then go on to create your own, composing poetry that you admire. A model provides a solid architectural plan or map, a way home, using effective tools and strategies. Simply list the devices and strategies that the poet employs and incorporate them into your own work. Modeling leaves content and tone decisions to the poet and simply offers us tactics that enhance our own writing.

TEN BASICS OF EFFECTIVE WRTING

PRE-WRITING WARM-UP

Give yourself permission to dream. Consider memories: places lived, important people, embarrassments, a lie you told, a hardship, a triumph, a failure, someone who bullied you, someone you helped or someone you admire. Tell your story from the point of view of a loved object: list specific specifics: names of songs, movies, shoes, jewelry, trips, or sports equipment. Try a cluster outline. Brainstorm. Try music. Select a topic and free write or read other poets to stimulate your writing. Some of us walk.

#1 Work first from your right brain, work small, start with a free write:

Select a vivid memory, then help the reader step into it. Explore multiple aspects. This isn't a logical or linear activity. Review rules for free writing: set a timer for seven minutes, always keep your hand moving, don't stop, don't edit, cross out, proofread or correct. Forget neat, grammar, and spelling for now, scribble, lose control and take risks, write from your heart not your head, avoid logic – leap. If it will help, write with crayons or colored markers. Order the disorder later. Go back and highlight vivid phrases and images, pull them out. Start again, rewrite in formal English, incorporate only the gems from your free write, get out of your mind first, then reclaim it as you proofread and edit.

#2 Be yourself.

Avoid gobble-de-gook and most abstract nouns! (Like truth, love & the American Way) Relax. Speak in your own voice. Don't work at being clever or erudite. No one wants to read or is fooled by writing that sounds like you are running from yourself. Have fun. Fall in love. Play. Make yourself and the world cry. How? Skip ahead to number three. Then remember: "*Fail, fail faster, fail better.*" Embrace your fear. I include below a five minute free write on failure:

Failure. Always and often -- the F+, the F, the F-. Why and how to avoid the label? All labels, the good-bad trap, the failure trap, the nonsense of what other people think, the tyranny of teachers and all the evaluations, the tyranny of culture, religion, education, family – even with the best of intentions. And then the not knowing, and then the "Am I good enough?" nonsense, the boot camps of evaluation, addictions to good girl and being right, and am I worthy? How to get out of this trap? A cage with the door open, which isn't a cage at all if you look at it properly and then just step out, then stay out.

#3 Show don't tell

See it, hear it, smell it, feel it, taste it, tell it like a film: use images. Show us a situation that evokes emotions; do not tell us about it. Effective writing is never plot summary. Help your writer live it. Use present tense. Trim excessive adjectives and all redundant adverbs, shun adverbs like slowly or loudly. Use images instead. Let us see it, feel it or hear it! Adverbs only tell and do not engage the reader. Avoid weak verbs of being such as: is, am or are. Stick with present tense action verbs: waltz, grovel, delight or howl.

#4 Use a narrative hook

Open with a hook or attention grabber. See the section on opening. Compelling dialogue or images work best. Invest much of your planning time on that initial hook, then focus on the conclusion and finally, add an epigraph and spend time on your title.

#5 Be specific and concrete; avoid abstractions.

Use lists. Avoid generalities. Write about the willow not trees and the hibiscus not a flower, refer to Nikes or stilettos not shoes. Do NOT pepper your writing with abstract nouns like love, truth, soul or honor. Use these words sparingly, at first, if at all. Evoke the feelings in your reader first without using these labels. Definitions are often fuzzy or personal. Again see #3. Show don't tell. Include specifics of geography, costume, time, food, music or character: use dialogue – describe habits and quirks.

#6 Use understatement not hyperbole

Avoid the angst-ridden sort of writing that makes many of us groan. Write honestly about pain but don't go for suffering. Revise hyperbolic phrases like "crying tears of blood" or melodrama. As the Dali Lama is reputed to have said "Pain is inevitable but suffering, optional." Convey it, but why wallow? If you need a good rant get out your journal and enjoy a *private* catharsis or seek therapy. Don't confuse art with therapy. (Or if you use hyperbole do it with awareness, for instance, use it for satire.)

 # 7 Style: Use PVC

Parallel structure, sentence **V**ariety and **C**onciseness. Many thanks to Kevin Coll, one of my son's teacher's, for this one. Sentence variety refers to the length of your sentences. Do not write a series of monotonous eight to ten word sentences. Vary the length! Mix short, simple sentences with complex or complex-compound sentences.

Read the entire rough draft, and revise it to include parallel structure, then reread and delete for conciseness, then rewrite for sentence variety. Reread again and delete another 25% your words. Done!

#8 Use figurative language, allusion and synesthesia, but sparingly

Experiment with a simile or metaphor or personification as well as literary or historical allusions or references. Mix your images: smell a sound or hear a feeling or taste a feeling as in the clichéd phrase, "I could taste his fear." Mix an abstraction (music) with a sense (feeling) as in, "the hard-blue music of a winter sleet storm" Go back and hone or add after you have an acceptable early draft and know both your focus and the structure.

#9 Locate an epigraph

Google *quotation.com* or other sites to find an appropriate epigraph. The epigraph for my last book of poetry, *Riffs,* is inscribed below using the proper form. No quotation marks are required, only italics with the author's name justified to the right of the text directly below the last line.

We must risk delight. We must have the stubbornness to accept our gladness in the ruthless furnace of this world.

--Jack Gilbert

#10 Revise, Revise, Revise

Not happy? Recycle. Try another topic, Free write again. Recycle. Diligence pays. Expect to put in time. Yes! Hours and hours. Expect to have fun exploring, defining and recreating your life and stories. *Slay your darlings*. Think of revision as a verbal slide show: a way to record, capture and savor. Use the Rough Draft Rubric and Revision Recipe. Recycle. Then finally, use the Revision Worksheet.

WORKSHEETS & CHECKLISTS

THE NAYLOR METHOD

It's not the strongest of the species that survives. Not the most intelligent that survives. It's the one that is most adaptable to change.
— Charles Darwin

- Select a model. Read it. Do a six minute free write, then a cluster brainstorm.
- Write a rough draft. Utilizing over 70% of your model's tips & instructions.
- Proofread for plagiarism! Use *only* strategies & techniques, not exact words.
- Incorporate best phrases from free write & your cluster brainstorm into your draft.
- Then evaluate with the Rough Draft Rubric. Revise again.
- Read aloud.
- Fill out the Revision Worksheet and Revision Recipe.
- Locate a sympathetic reader or workshop. Share your piece.
- Revise again. Incorporate only the feedback that feels right.
- Read aloud, again. Tweak it. Take it to a workshop.
- Revise again & submit for publication.

Two Practical Publication Tips:

If you have a promising poem that has been well-revised and work-shopped, consider adding the literary device synesthesia to the poem. Look it up in the glossary. Or for any short prose contests, submit a well-honed poem. Simply reformat it, turning your poetic lines into paragraphs.

STUCK? REVIEW YOUR PROCESS

Be Yourself, Breathe. Relax.

Try a cluster outline.

Then free write for seven minutes. Review the free write rules.

Organize parts (list anecdotes and examples on index cards.) Shuffle to reorder.

Show don't tell. Employ mostly nouns and verbs. Avoid adjectives or adverbs.

See it, hear it, smell it, feel it, taste it, could it be a film? Use images & dialogue.

Be ruthless in editing excess or redundant words.

Develop your ear. Read aloud.

Read fine writers. A list is provided.

Read your work aloud to yourself first. Then revise.

Use figurative language sparingly. Do not confuse your reader or yourself.

When in doubt use plain diction not ornate,

Stick with the Anglo-Saxon. Avoid more intellectual Latinate based words.

Practice sentence variety. Then arrange in stanzas. Consider line breaks.

After free write, invest initial writing in conceiving hook, conclusion and title.

Locate an epigraph. Google quotation.com

Strive to be consistently clear, brief and bold.

Get feedback from supportive readers. Workshop it.

ROUGH DRAFT RUBRIC

1. **Techniques** (5 points)

___Specific details (furniture) use of at least one allusion	1
___Image or sensory-based, concrete not abstract, show don't tell	1
___Language: diction, dialogue, fluid, syntax, no chopped prose	1
___Figurative Language: metaphor, symbol, personification, simile	1
___Sound/music: anaphora, rhyme, alliteration, assonance, tone conforms	.5
___Voice: author in control of subject and tone	.5

   ___**TOTAL (5)**

2. **Mechanics**: (2 points)
   Punctuation, sentence errors, spelling, line breaks, usage, tense or POV changes, pronouns, agreement, usage, epigraphs punctuated, present tense, active verbs!
   ___**TOTAL (2)**

3. **Coherence:** Clear focus: title, content & format reinforce one another
   ___**TOTAL (1)**

4. **Style:** Plain, sentence variety, parallel structure, concise, panache
   ___**TOTAL (1)**

5. **Manuscript Style**:
   No bold or centering, 12 pt. fonts, Times New Roman, spacing 1.5 poetry & 2 for prose, CAPS for titles, margins left, no auto caps
   ___**TOTAL (1)**

   ___Epigraphs: extra credit + 2 out of 100

   ___**GRAND TOTAL (10)**

   COMMENTS:

GRADE A, FIRST-CLASS, TOP-NOTCH, SURE-FIRE, REVISION RECIPE

___1. Check off or add an epigraph below your title and before the text.

___2. Use at least one literary, artistic, historical, scientific allusion or reference.

___3. Figurative language: add metaphor, synesthesia, oxymoron or paradox.

___4. Upgrade vocabulary of three words. Use a thesaurus but don't overdo!

　　　Replace verbs of being with action verbs. Avoid "am," "is" or "are" verbs.

___5. Use two lists for music and momentum.

___6. Use an auditory image, add an additional image, one should not be visual.

___7. Read aloud. Listen for sound. Consider euphony, cacophony, refrains.

Incorporate PVC:

___8. Parallel structure: *I came. I saw. I conquered.* Or *Of the people, by the....*

___9. Conciseness: trim any extra words. Avoid redundancy.

___10. Use sentence variety. Vary short sentences or frags. Combine two

　　　short sentences to achieve a more complex expression.

Other:

Ask the "so what?" & "who cares?" questions. Mentor. Does your work startle our delight? If not try again. Use irony. Proofread for unity, logic & coherence. Check facts. Do a little research. Volunteer to give & get help from peer editor.

REVISION WORKSHEET

___1. Use at least (one more) allusion. New allusion =_____.

___2. Figurative language: simile, metaphor, personification, synesthesia, paradox, or oxymoron. Quote two examples that you added to the back of this paper.

___3. Add at least one hyphenated sentence or phrase. Copy it on the back.

___4. Upgrade the vocabulary of three ho-hum words. Use a thesaurus. Add _____, _____, & _____.

___5. Use two more lists for music and momentum. Name the types of lists: ie, rivers, sea shells, shoes, birds, hobbies _____ & _____.

___6. Add two new images, one should not be visual. List _____ & _____.

___7. Consciously used sound: employ anaphora, rhyme, alliteration, euphony or cacophony. Quote on the back of this paper.

___8. Employee parallel structure. (Practice the sacred art of PVC: #'s 8-10 below) Parallel structure = "I came. I saw. I conquered." List yours on back.

___9. Be concise. Trim extra words. Cross out three words on your rough draft. List extras here. _____, _____, & _____.

___10. Use sentence variety. Compose a short sentence, then combine several complex-compound sentences. Vary. Intersperse a few one-word sentences or fragments. Wake up your reader. Sentences of the same length = monotony. Vary your syntax. See glossary for any definitions you require.

GLOSSARY OF LITERARY TERMS

ALLITERATION = repetition of initial consonant sounds.

    Example: Peter Piper picked a peck of pickled peppers.

ASSONANCE= repetition of vowel sounds. Example: The loud howl of the owl.

ALLUSION = a reference to an historical, mythological, literary, artistic or scientific event

    fact or person.

    Examples: Apollo, Einstein, Napoleon, the Gettysburg Address, Darwin, Picasso, Shakespeare's sonnets, Pearl Harbor, the Eiffel Tower, the Crimean War.

ANACHONISM = something outside its historical context.

    Example: A helicopter flies over the battle of Gettysburg.

ANAPHORA = a refrain or repetition of single words usually at the beginning of a phrase.

    Example: I remember Paris, I remember Jean Val jean, I remember the Louvre, ...

CACOPHONY = harsh, grading sounds.

    Example: clickety-clack or screech.

DICTION = word choice,

    Example: The dictions of professor and beggar vary dramatically.

DIDACTIC = intending to instruct,

    Example: preachers, teachers and parents are often didactic.

ELEGY = a poem written to praise the dead.

EPIGRAPH = a guiding quotation that is placed beneath the title and before the text. It should have relevance to your topic the words are italicized – no quotation marks are necessary since the author's name is placed below the quotation. Put a dash in front of the author's name and line up the last letter of his or her name with the last letter in the quotation.

Example:

ACERBIC WIT: A BIOGRAPHY	title
Living well is the best revenge.	quotation
– Oscar Wilde	author

EUPHONY = the use of soothing and harmonious sounds.

Example: The sweet susurrations of a loon.

FREE WRITE = It's important to know that writing poetry is often more emotional than cognitive. Recognize also that the two are often inextricable. This is where the value of a free write emerges. Do it. Don't over think it. Fire your internal editor. Just dabble and play. Surrender to your right brain, start with a seven minute free write. Instructions below.

Select a vivid memory. Step into it. Be there. Explore multiple aspects. This isn't a logical or linear activity. Set a timer for seven minutes, then keep your hand moving, don't stop, don't edit, cross out, proofread or correct. If you can't think of anything to say write, "I can't think of anything to say" until you do. Dive into your subconscious. Forget neat, forget grammar, and spelling for now, scribble, lose control and take risks, write from your heart not your head, avoid logic – leap. If it helps, write with crayons or colored markers or non-dominant hand.

Order the disorder later. When you finish, go back and highlight vivid phrases or images, pull them out. Start again, rewrite in formal English, incorporate only the gems from your free write, get out of your mind first, proofread and edit later.

HYPERBOLE = exaggeration.

    Example: the traffic jam almost killed me.

IMAGERY = the incorporation of our five senses in writing.

    Example: Employ visual, taste, smell, auditory or kinesthetic (feeling) senses

IRONY= the unexpected. There are three types: verbal, situational and dramatic.

Verbal= saying the opposite of what you mean, often used in sarcasm.

Example: I just love mildew.

Situational = when an unexpected situation occurs,

Example: a firehouse burns down or a cop is handcuffed to a police car.

Dramatic = always involves an unexpected ignorance.

Example: in the drama, *Oedipus Rex*, the King searches for a murderer but is ignorant of the fact that he unwittingly murdered his own father, then marries his mother. Whew!

LINES = Some say this is the only concrete or measurable thing that separates a poem from prose. Prose is written between the margins of a piece of paper, a machine or your hand fills this space with words, while the poet determines and controls line length in a poem. The poet determines what line length serves his purpose best. Dickinson wrote small cramped lines, reflecting her ideas and disposition, while Whitman wrote his *Song of the Open Road* in long, expansive, loping, almost prose-like lines. When your form reflects the content the reader receives a more coherent message. It's up to you to experiment with lines and determine whether you will stick with a signature line length or vary it depending upon your content. Lines may end at the end of a sentence or phrase or clause or it may be enjambed or dropped down and wrapped into the next line as in the lines */all fall/*

down./

Enjambment is a special tool best utilized by the proficient. Avoid it early on as well as the heavy-handed use of rhymed couplets or end rhyme which produces a sing-song, Dr. Seuss or Hallmark card tone or effect. If you do employ these devices it's prudent to get feedback from those whose work you respect.

LISTS = a series of specifics that provide texture and call up a variety of connotations. Below is a short list poem I wrote consisting of a series of names.

MELTING POT

Faizaan, Avrumie, Salomon, Jaime, Qi An, Javi.

I savor the alien sounds of my teaching, turned gypsy,
gone are all those Tom, Dick and Harry's,
as I, still somewhat stationary,
merge with immigrant, with movement, crises,
with change, as cultures, eras, institutions,
insist on the dynamic, the vital,
the fluid, chanting our new song:

Qi An, Jaime, Avrumie, Javi, Salomon, Faizaan.

METAPHOR = an indirect comparison, such as "the rose-fingered dawn"

MODEL = a recipe or set of instructions derived from a successful poem. The model, analyzes strategies so students may select and duplicate techniques while incorporating their own content, diction and tone. See the section titled Six Models for many examples.

ONOMATOPEOIA = when a word sounds like the thing it describes.

    Examples: buzz, rasp, hiss, shush, whisper, cuckoo, slurp, etc.

PARALLEL STRUCTURE = a series of grammatically similar phrases

    Example: "of the people, by the people, for the people" repeats a series of prepositional phrases or consider "His writing a comedy, his life a tragedy, Oscar Wilde…." The parallel is in the repetition of a phrase that starts with a pronoun, then a noun, an article and finally, another noun or remember Caesar's famous line: "I came. I saw. I conquered." Here three first person pronouns (I) are followed by the three past tense verbs: "came, saw, and conquered."

PARADOX= an apparent contradiction.

    Example: "Parting is such sweet sorrow." or the phrase, living death.

PROMPT= a writing assignment

    Example: Describe your family's front porch when you were twelve.

SATIRE = to ridicule institutions or powerful people with either the intention of improving society or just for fun or for the entertainment value.

SIMILE = a direct comparison using like or as. This is less subtle than the metaphor.

    Example: the dawn looks like a series of rose-colored fingers.

SYMBOL = when one thing stands for or represents another.

Example: You are as American as apple pie. Apple pie = America

SYNESTHESIA = a mixing of two of the five senses.

Examples: I could taste his fear. OR The heat of her voice mesmerized us.

SYNTAX = refers to word order. Vary the structure of your sentences.

Example: Do not automatically use the standard formula of subject/ verb /object, as in "I waltz with fairies." Try instead to use an introductory phrase or clause like "Only after waking, do I waltz with the fairies."

Experiment with a bit of playful taxsyn. Suit yourself, nothing else. Really matters. It does. Not. Matter. Yo ho ho & a bottle of fun. Break one rule a day. Get' over. It... (note to editor. Leave this alone!)

TONE= the mood or emotional attitude of an author or literary work.

UNDERSTATEMENT = minimizing or downplaying a situation. Opposite of hyperbole.

Example: Her grief was minor.

SUGGESTED READING

Writing Texts:

Bird by Bird, Anne Lamott & *Poemcrazy* by Susan Wooldridge

Writing Down the Bones, also *Wild Minds,* Natalie Goldberg

Writing Toward Home, Georgia Heard & *You Are a Writer,* Jeff Goins

The Idiot's Guide to Writing Poetry, Nikki Moustakki & *Ordinary Genius,* Kim Addonizio,

The Poets Companion, Kim Addonizio & Dorianne Laux

Poetry Collections:

Any by Billy Collins, Galway Kinnell, Robert Hass, Mary Oliver, Jim Daniels, Maxine Kumin, Campbell McGrath, Tony Hoagland, Gerald Stern, Jack Gilbert, Richard Blanco, Barbara Hamby, David Kirby, Mark Halliday, David Rivard, Stephen Dunn, Tess Gallagher, Bob Hicok, Mark Cox, Naomi Shihab Nye, Heather McHugh, Linda Gregg. Stanley Plummley, Czeslaw Milosz, William Stafford, Mark Strand, Sharon Olds, Charles Simic or Thomas Lux.

Anthologies: *Best Poems of 2016* or any from the last five years.

Online journals: *Rattle* & *SOFLOPOJO*, South Florida Poetry Journal(monthly)

Prose: Stories by Barry Lopez, Ellen Gilchrist or memoir by Annie Dillard.

POEMS REPRINTED

Jan Heller Levi, *Not Bad Dad, Not Bad*

Jeffrey Delotto, *Cicadas*

Yusef Komunakka, *Venus's Fly Trap*

Logan Funderburk, *How to Laugh Like A Mad Scientist*

Holly Iglesias, *Perishables*

Catherine Scott, *Road Music: I-75 Getting Away To The Middle Of Nowhere*

Campbell McGrath, *Sunset, Route 90, Brewster County, Texas*

Any unattributed work is my own.

AUTHOR PROFILE

Sally Naylor, perennial gypsy, is also a teacher, therapist and wordsmith. She enjoys photography and the water birds on her lake in Coral Springs, Florida. Sally taught and wrote curricula for gifted, creative writing, peer counseling and AIDS education classes at both Ransom Everglades and the Baylor School. She received awards in poetry and creative non-fiction in the FIU MFA program. Today poetry workshops, interviews, travel, yoga, roller derby, gymnastics, alligator and arm wrestling keep her out of trouble. Mostly.

Her poetry collections, *Firebird, Heresies & Sweet Basil* and *Riffs* (PP Books) are available online, as is her memoir, *Rogue Nirvana* (Lioncrest Press) She took the lead in editing an anthology of her Broward County, Florida poetry workshop, *Slay Your Darlings: An Anthology by the No Name Poets,* (PP Books) December, 2016. She currently is composing a creative writing text for busy professionals as well as a self-help book : *The Schlepp Factor.*

First Light provides a commonsense guide for any committed rookie poet. This first volume of Naylor's curricula presents initial models as well as a mindset that will jumpstart your success.   Look for further volumes of *First Light* in 2019.

THE PETER PAN DINER

There's a hell of a universe next door. Let's go.

Let's celebrate after the storm,

as hysteria defers and eulogies slowly wind down.

For soon the double arch rainbow will paint itself above the Peter Pan Diner.

So magical realism. So miracle. So now.

A salute from this open-sesame, zigzag season.

Ta Da.

After I outgrew my Seven League Boots,

having lost track finally, of the score —

with much space and gratitude –

for all so-called "mountains" climbed.

I now hook both thumbs in the straps

of my imaginary Lederhosen and exhort:

You too, pilgrim. Join me.

Pick your galaxy. Step up.

Turn left at the North Star.

www.ingramcontent.com/pod-product-compliance
Lightning Source LLC
Chambersburg PA
CBHW081727100526
44591CB00016B/2532